LEBANESE COOKBOOK

MAIN COURSE – 60 + Quick and easy to prepare at home recipes, step-by-step guide to the classic Lebanese cuisine

TABLE OF CONTENTS

purposes solely, and is universal as so. The presentation of the information is without contract or any type of guarantee assurance.

The trademarks that are used are without any consent, and the publication of the trademark is without permission or backing by the trademark owner. All trademarks and brands within this book are for clarifying purposes only and are the owned by the owners themselves, not affiliated with this document.

Introduction

Lebanese recipes for personal enjoyment but also for family enjoyment. You will love them for sure for how easy it is to prepare them.

SHAKSHUKA

Serves: **2**
Prep Time: **15**   Minutes

Cook Time: **20**   Minutes

Total Time: **35**   Minutes

INGREDIENTS

- 4 eggs
- 3 tbs parsley
- 1 red capsicum
- 2 tomatoes
- 14 oz crushed tomatoes
- ½ cup chicken broth
- 1 ½ tsp paprika
- ½ tsp black pepper
- 1 red onion
- 2 tbs olive oil
- 1 tsp cumin

- 2 tbs tomato paste
- 2 garlic cloves
- 1/3 tsp salt

DIRECTIONS

1. Cook the onion and garlic in hot oil for about 3 minutes
2. Add in the capsicum and cook for another minute
3. Add the diced tomatoes, cook for about 2 minutes, then add the canned tomatoes, broth, tomato paste, cumin, paprika, salt, and pepper
4. Simmer on low for 5 minutes, then crack the eggs in and cook for 1-2 minutes
5. Bake in the preheated oven for about 10 minutes at 350F
6. Serve immediately

Serves: **4**

Prep Time: **2**   Hours

Cook Time: **15** Minutes

Total Time: **2**   Hours

INGREDIENTS

- Naan manousheh
- 4 cups flour
- 1 cup yogurt
- ½ cup warm water
- Za'tar
- Akkawi cheese
- 1 ½ tbs sugar
- 1 cup boiling water
- 3 tsp oil
- 3 tsp dry yeast
- 1 ½ tsp salt

DIRECTIONS

1. Mix the yeast with sugar and warm water
2. Mix the yogurt and the boiling water
3. Add the yeast and 3 cups of flour and mix well
4. Leave to rest covered for at least 30 minutes
5. Add the salt, oil and slowly the remaining flour, kneading well for about 5 minutes
6. Place covered in a warm place until it doubles in size
7. Divide the dough in 6 portions
8. Roll the dough into discs and cook into medium hot oil
9. Brush with butter after 3 minutes
10. Flip over and top with desired topping
11. Fold it in half and cook for 1 minute on each side
12. Serve immediately

POTATOES AND EGGS

Serves: **6**

Prep Time: **15** Minutes

Cook Time: **1** Hour

Total Time: **1** Hour

INGREDIENTS

- 8 eggs
- 3 tbs olive oil
- 3 tbs herbs
- 2 onions
- 3 lb potatoes
- Salt
- Pepper

DIRECTIONS

1. Cook the onions for about 3 minutes in hot oil
2. Reduce the heat and simmer, stirring every 10 minutes for 30 minutes
3. Spread the diced potatoes in a colander and toss with salt, then let sit for about 5 minutes

4. Rinse with cold water
5. Stir the potatoes over the onions adding salt and herbs
6. Cook covered a little more until soft
7. Stir in the eggs and cook until done
8. Serve immediately

SPICED SAUSAGES

Serves: *3*

Prep Time: *10*   Minutes

Cook Time: *20*   Minutes

Total Time: *30*   Minutes

INGREDIENTS

- 8 eggs
- 8 oz minced lamb
- 8 oz minced beef
- 2 tbs lemon juice
- 1 tsp cloves
- 3 tsp coriander
- 3 tsp pepper
- 3 tsp coriander
- 4 tbs pine nuts
- 3 tsp pepper
- 1 tsp nutmeg
- 1 red chilli
- 3 garlic cloves
- 2 tsp salt

- 2 inch piece ginger
- 5 tbs wine
- 3 tbs oil

DIRECTIONS

1. Place the lamb and the beef into a bowl and season with coriander, pepper, salt, ginger, chilli, nutmeg, pine nuts, cloves, garlic, and white wine
2. Mix well and marinate overnight
3. Shape the meat dough into sausages
4. Cook in hot oil for at least 5 minutes
5. Crack the eggs over the sausages and cook until done
6. Serve with tomatoes or fresh greens

Serves: **4**

Prep Time: **10** Minutes

Cook Time: **40** Minutes

Total Time: **50** Minutes

INGREDIENTS

- 1 cup chickpeas
- 1/3 cup pine nuts
- 3 cloves garlic
- 3 tbs butter
- 1 loaf Lebanese bread
- 450g Greek yogurt

DIRECTIONS

1. Soak the chickpeas in water overnight
2. Drain the chickpeas and rinse with water, then place in a water filled saucepan
3. Bring to a boil, then reduce the heat and simmer for about 30 minutes

14

4. Strain the chickpeas, reserving a little bit of the liquid and season with salt, then stir to combine and set aside

5. Toast the bread until golden and crumble into smaller pieces

6. Crush the garlic with salt until it becomes a paste, then add the yogurt and mix well

7. Toast the pine nuts until they change color, then add the butter and cook until browned

8. Spread a layer of bread, then top with chickpeas, yogurt and pine nuts

9. Serve immediately

ZUCCHINI OMELET

Serves: **2**

Prep Time: **5**   Minutes

Cook Time: **5**   Minutes

Total Time: **10**   Minutes

INGREDIENTS

- 4 eggs
- 1 ½ tsp salt
- 2 zucchinis
- Olive oil
- 1 cup parsley
- 1 pinch pepper
- 1 onion

DIRECTIONS

1. Grate zucchini
2. Mix the ingredients together in a bowl except the eggs
3. Beat the eggs separately and combine with the mixture

4. Pour the mixture in heated oil and fry for 3 minutes per side

5. Serve with pita

Serves: *4*
Prep Time: *5*   Minutes

Cook Time: *10*   Minutes

Total Time: *15*   Minutes

INGREDIENTS

- 3 tbs pine nuts
- 1/3 lb ground lamb
- 2 tbs oil
- 1/3 cup onion
- 2 cloves garlic
- 2 tsp spices seasoning
- 2 tbs green scalions
- 4 eggs
- Salt

DIRECTIONS

1. Cook the onion in oil for 5 minutes

2. Add the lamb and the garlic, then season with the spices and cook until browned

3. Pour the beaten eggs over and cook until done

4. Top with toasted pine nuts and serve

HALLOUMI AND EGGS

Serves: **2**
Prep Time: **5**   Minutes

Cook Time: **10**   Minutes

Total Time: **15**   Minutes

INGREDIENTS

- Olive oil
- 4 eggs
- tbs Greek yogurt
- Mint
- 4 slices halloumi
- Paprika

DIRECTIONS

1. Cook the haloumi in hot oil until brown
2. Crack the eggs over
3. Season with paprika and cook until done
4. Mix the yogurt with chopped mint and drizzle over the egg

5. Serve hot

Serves: **4**

Prep Time: **10** Minutes

Cook Time: **10** Minutes

Total Time: **20** Minutes

INGREDIENTS

- 6 eggs
- 1 tsp allspice
- 1 tomato
- 1 potato
- 2 tsp water
- 3 tbs oil
- 1 onion
- 1 bunch spinach
- 1 zucchini
- 1/3 eggplant
- 1 bell pepper
- 10 mushrooms
- Salt
- Pepper

DIRECTIONS

1. Sauté the onions in oil for a few minutes, then add the potato

2. Cook for a few more minutes

3. Add the eggplant and season with salt and pepper

4. Add the mushrooms, zucchini and peppers one at a time

5. Whisk together the eggs, water and allspice and pour over the mixture

6. Add the tomato and the spinach when the eggs are almost ready

7. Serve immediately

Serves: *4*
Prep Time: *10*   Minutes

Cook Time: *15*   Minutes

Total Time: *25*   Minutes

INGREDIENTS

- 6 eggs
- 1/3 cup parsley leaves
- 2 tbs olive oil
- 1 tsp salt
- 5 cherry tomatoes
- 3 tsp lemon juice
- 1 tsp harissa
- 1 tbs mint leaves
- 16 pita chips
- 1 tsp cumin
- 10 oz potatoes
- 2 scallions

DIRECTIONS

1. Mix 1 tbs oil, harissa, lemon juice, cumin and a pinch of salt together

2. Slice the potatoes and toss into the mixture

3. Cook the potato slices in the hot remaining oil until browned

4. Add the white part of the scallions and sauté for about 3 minutes

5. Add the tomatoes, beaten eggs, parsley, green part of the scallions, mint, and another pinch of salt and cook for another 2 minutes

6. Stir in the chips

7. Serve immediately

LUNCH

LEBANESE LENTIL SOUP

Serves: *4*
Prep Time: *10* Minutes

Cook Time: *50* Minutes

Total Time: *60* Minutes

INGREDIENTS

- 2 tbs olive oil
- 1 ½ tsp cinnamon
- 2 stalks celery
- 4 cloves garlic
- 3 tsp cumin
- 1 onion
- 2 carrots
- 1 cup lentils
- 4 cups chicken broth
- 6 cups spinach
- 4 cups water
- 1 lemon

- Salt
- Pepper

DIRECTIONS

1. Cook the carrots, onions and celery in hot oil until tender
2. Season with salt and pepper
3. Add garlic, cinnamon and cumin and heat for 1 minute
4. Stir in the lentils and heat for about 2 minutes
5. Pour in the water, chicken broth and lemon juice and bring to a boil
6. Summer for at least 30 minutes
7. Stir in the spinach and cook for 2 more minutes
8. Season and serve

CHICKPEA SOUP

Serves: **6**
Prep Time: **10** Minutes

Cook Time: **30** Minutes

Total Time: **40** Minutes

INGREDIENTS

- 3 tbs olive oil
- 1 ½ tsp paprika powder
- 2 bay leaves
- 1 onion
- 2 tomatoes
- 3 tbs tomato paste
- 1 lemon
- 1 handful parsley
- 1 cup water
- 3 cups vegetable broth
- 2 cups chickpeas
- 2 carrots
- 3 potato
- ½ tsp chili flakes

- 2 tbs yeast
- 3 garlic cloves

Baharat powder:

- 1/3 tsp cinnamon
- 1/3 tsp nutmeg
- ½ tsp cloves
- 1 tsp coriander

- ½ tsp cardamom
- 1 tsp ginger powder
- 2 tsp red peppercorns

DIRECTIONS

1. Roast the Barhat spices for about a minute
2. Saute the garlic and onions in hot oil for 2 minutes until soft
3. Add in the diced tomatoes and cook for 3 more minutes, then add the potatoes and carrots
4. Add in the powder and bay leaves and cook for a few more minutes
5. Add the tomato paste, broth, chili flakes, paprika powder and water and bring to a boil
6. Add in the boiled chickpeas
7. Simmer for at least 5 minutes
8. Remove from heat and stir in the lemon juice and chopped parsley

9. Let it rest and serve

VEGETABLE SOUP

Serves: *8*
Prep Time: *10*   Minutes

Cook Time: *30*   Minutes

Total Time: *40*   Minutes

INGREDIENTS

- 10 artichokes
- 2 onions
- ½ tsp salt
- 1/3 cup parsley
- 3 tbs olive oil
- 2 cups potatoes
- 5 cups vegetable stock
- 3 garlic cloves
- 3 cups carrots
- 1 cup chickpeas
- 2 tomatoes
- 2 lemon
- 1/3 tsp red pepper
- 1 tsp coriander

DIRECTIONS

1. Sauté the onions in hot oil for about 5 minutes

2. Stir in the carrots and cook a little more covered

3. Season with coriander, pepper and garlic, then cook a few more minutes

4. Add the potatoes, 2 cups of stock and salt

5. Cover and bring to a boil

6. Simmer until tender

7. Stir in the chickpeas, artichoke hearts and tomatoes and season with salt

8. Simmer for around 3 minutes, then pour in the stock

9. Serve sprinkled with parsley

CHICKEN AND VERMICELLI SOUP

Serves: *6*
Prep Time: *10* Minutes

Cook Time: *20* Minutes

Total Time: *30* Minutes

INGREDIENTS

- 3 lb chicken parts
- 2 carrots
- 2 lemons
- ¾ cup vermicelli noodles
- 1 celery stick
- 1 onion
- 2 bay leaves
- 2 cloves garlic
- Salt
- Pepper
- Cinnamon

DIRECTIONS

1. Gently brown the chicken in a pot, then add cold water, carrots, onion and celery stick

2. Bring to a boil, covered

3. Simmer for at least 1 hour, then cool and strain the broth

4. Store the broth in fridge

5. Break the chicken meat in little pieces and cover

6. Heat the broth, add the vermicelli and bring to a boil for 3 minutes

7. Add the chicken meat and serve topped with parsley and cinnamon

GREEN SPLIT PEA SOUP

Serves: *4*
Prep Time: *20* Minutes

Cook Time: *40* Minutes

Total Time: *60* Minutes

INGREDIENTS

- 2 tbs olive oil
- 2 stalks celery
- 1 tsp black pepper
- 5 cloves garlic
- 4 potatoes
- 1 onion
- 3 tsp cumin
- 3 cups vegetable broth
- ½ cup parsley
- 1 lemon
- 1 ½ cups green split peas

DIRECTIONS

1. Boil the chickpeas in water for about 15 minutes, then drain and set aside

2. Place the peeled potatoes in cold, salted water and bring to a boil cooking for almost 10 minutes

3. Sauté the onions and garlic in hot oil for about 5 minutes

4. Season with pepper, cumin and salt

5. Add in the potatoes, split peas, celery and vegetable broth, then bring to a boil and reduce to simmer until fully cooked

6. Puree the soup using a blender until smooth

7. Serve immediately

EGGPLANT GANOUSH

Serves: *8*
Prep Time: *30* Minutes

Cook Time: *20* Minutes

Total Time: *50* Minutes

INGREDIENTS

- 550 g eggplant
- 3 tbs olive oil
- 1/3 cup lemon juice
- 2 garlic cloves
- 1 tsp sumac
- 1/3 cup parsley leaves
- 1 ½ tsp salt
- 450 g lentils

DIRECTIONS

1. Cook the eggplant in a chargrill pan until tender, then set aside to cool
2. Peel the eggplant and place in a food processor

3. Add lemon juice, oil, parsley, salt, garlic, ½ tsp sumac and the lentils reserving 2 tbs of them

4. Pulse until combined and chunky

5. Serve sprinkled with lentils

KEBABS ON COUSCOUS

Serves: **4**

Prep Time: **10**   Minutes

Cook Time: **20**   Minutes

Total Time: **30**   Minutes

INGREDIENTS

- 6 chicken thighs
- 200 g cherry tomatoes
- 1/3 cup mint
- 1 cup couscous
- 3 tbs olive oil
- 1 ½ tbs sumac
- 1/3 cup lemon juice
- 1 cup parsley leaves
- 2 green onions
- 3 garlic cloves
- ½ tsp coriander
- 1 cup chicken stock

DIRECTIONS

1. Mix chicken, sumac, garlic, coriander and half of the oil together
2. Season with salt and pepper and thread the chicken onto skewers
3. Cook the chicken skewers on a chargrill pan until golden
4. Pour the chicken stock into a saucepan and bring to a boil
5. Remove from heat and add the couscous
6. Set aside covered for 5 minutes
7. Transfer to a bowl and add mint, parsley, tomatoes, lemon juice, onion and the remaining oil
8. Mix well then season with salt and pepper
9. Serve the couscous topped with the kebabs

SHISH CHICKEN

Serves: *4*
Prep Time: *10* Minutes

Cook Time: *10* Minutes

Total Time: *20* Minutes

INGREDIENTS

- 20 oz chicken breast
- ½ tsp pepper
- 3 cloves garlic
- 1 ½ tsp salt
- 1 ½ tbs olive oil
- 1 lemon

DIRECTIONS

1. In a bowl add the zest and juice of the lemon, salt, pepper and minced garlic, then place the cubed chicken in
2. Refrigerate overnight to marinate
3. Cook the chicken and the marinade in hot oil in a pan for about 5 minutes

4. Serve topped with parsley

CHICKEN AND POTATOES

Serves: *6*
Prep Time: *10*   Minutes

Cook Time: *50*   Minutes

Total Time: *60*   Minutes

INGREDIENTS

- 5 cloves garlic
- 8 chicken pieces
- ¾ cup lemon juice
- 8 potatoes
- ½ cup olive oil
- Salt
- Pepper

DIRECTIONS

1. Place the chicken and potatoes in a baking dish and season with salt and pepper
2. Mix the lemon juice, garlic and olive oil and pour the mixture over the chicken and potatoes

3. Cover the dich with a foil and place in the preheated oven

4. Bake for about 30 minutes at 200F, then remove foil and cook for 30 more minutes at 250F

5. Serve immediately

Serves: *4*
Prep Time: *10*   Minutes

Cook Time: *30*   Minutes

Total Time: *40*   Minutes

INGREDIENTS

- 2 lbs chicken
- 5 oz Greek yogurt
- 1 lemon
- ½ tsp honey
- 1 tbs oregano
- 1 tsp cumin
- 2 tbs garlic
- 1 tbs paprika
- Salt
- Pepper

DIRECTIONS

1. Mix everything together except for the chicken
2. Add in the chicken and allow to marinate for at least 3 hours
3. Place the chicken on baking sheet and cook in the preheated oven at 300F for at least 30 minutes
4. Allow to rest, then serve

DINNER

STUFFED PEPPERS

Serves: **4**

Prep Time: **40** Minutes

Cook Time: **30** Minutes

Total Time: **70** Minutes

INGREDIENTS

- 4 bell peppers
- ½ cup parsley
- 3 tsp olive oil
- ¼ tsp sugar
- ½ tsp oregano
- 1 tsp black pepper
- 1 cup tomatoes
- 1/3 cup water
- ¾ cup beef broth
- 1 lb sirloin
- 2 cups water
- ¼ tsp red pepper

- 1 cup onion
- 2 tsp garlic
- 1 tsp salt
- 1/3 tsp cinnamon
- 3 tbs yogurt
- 1 cup rice
- 1 tsp allspice

DIRECTIONS

1. Cut the tops off bell peppers and reserve them
2. Discard seeds and place in a baking dish covered with paper towels
3. Microwave for 5 minutes on high, then allow to rest
4. Mix ½ tsp black pepper, ¼ cup broth, rice, allspice, cinnamon, salt and sirloin
5. Divide the mixture among peppers and top with the tops
6. Cover with water and bake at 450 for about 40 minutes
7. Sauté the onion in hot oil for at least 5 minutes, then add garlic and sauté 30 more seconds
8. Add black pepper, tomatoes, broth, water, sugar, red pepper, and oregano and bring to a boil
9. Reduce the heat and simmer for 30 minutes
10. Serve with lemon wedges

Serves: **4**
Prep Time: **20**   Minutes

Cook Time: **10**   Minutes

Total Time: **30**   Minutes

INGREDIENTS

- 450 g hummus
- 2 bunch mint
- 450 g Greek yogurt
- 1 onion
- 4 Lebanese bread
- 5 tsp olive oil
- 2 bag rocket leaves
- 5 cloves garlic
- 2 packet ground lamb
- 2 tsp vinegar
- 2 tsp cumin
- 1 ½ tsp paprika

DIRECTIONS

1. Chop the mint leaves, slice the onion, peel and crush the garlic and peel and grate the carrot

2. Mix Greek yogurt, vinegar and mint together, then season with salt and pepper

3. Cook the onion in hot oil for 5 minutes, then add the garlic, cumin and paprika and cook for 1 more minute

4. Add the meat and carrot and cook for another 5 minutes

5. Spread the hummus over each bread and then top with the meat mixture

6. Add the rocket leaves and roll them up

7. Heat in a pan for 3 minutes and serve

CHICKEN PASTA

Serves: **6**

Prep Time: **20** Minutes

Cook Time: **30** Minutes

Total Time: **50** Minutes

INGREDIENTS

- 2 chicken breasts
- 3 cups pasta
- 3 cups chicken broth
- 2 zucchinis
- 3 tbs basil
- 1/3 cup olive oil
- 10 tbs salt
- 3 tbs garlic
- 2 peppers
- 2 potatoes
- 1 onion
- 1 cup cherry tomatoes

- 5 tbs parmesan cheese

DIRECTIONS

1. Peel, chop and prepare the vegetables
2. Cook the potatoes in hot oil for 10 minutes
3. Add the zucchini and cook for 3 more minutes, then add the chicken and cook for 5 more minutes
4. Add the onions and peppers and cook 2 more minutes
5. Season with salt, basil and garlic, add ¼ cup oil, chicken broth, and rice
6. Cook for 10 minutes on high
7. Toss in the tomatoes
8. Serve topped with parmesan cheese

CINNAMON CHICKEN RICE

Serves: **10**
Prep Time: **20**   Minutes

Cook Time: **40**   Minutes

Total Time: **60**   Minutes

INGREDIENTS

- 1 chicken
- 1 onion
- 1 handful mint
- 2 cups labneh
- 1 ½ cinnamon sticks
- 1 pinch salt
- 1 cup raisins
- 1 cup almonds
- 3 cups rice
- 4 tbs cinnamon
- 1 ½ cups pomegranate seeds
- 1 stick butter
- ¾ cup pine nuts
- 2 bay leaves

DIRECTIONS

1. Cover the chicken with water and bring to a boil, then reduce the heat to a simmer

2. Cook for at least 20 minutes until tender, then set aside

3. Strain the broth into a bowl

4. Place the rice in 6 cups of broth and bring to a boil

5. Simmer covered for at least 15 minutes until done

6. Sauté the nuts in melted butter until golden

7. Mix rice, chicken, salt, raisins, cinnamon, half of the pine nuts, and almonds

8. Mix until well coated

9. Serve topped with remaining nuts, seeds, mint, and parsley

BEEF AND GREENS

Serves: *8*

Prep Time: *10*   Minutes

Cook Time: *20*   Minutes

Total Time: *30*   Minutes

INGREDIENTS

- 2 tbs olive oil
- 5 cloves garlic
- 1 lb ground beef
- 2 tbs Worcestershire sauce
- 3 tbs red wine
- 2 tbs butter
- 1 lb green beans
- 25 oz tomato sauce
- 2 tsp salt
- 1 tsp black pepper
- 1 onion

DIRECTIONS

1. Cook the onions in warm butter and oil for 5 minutes

2. Add the garlic and sauté for 30 seconds

3. Add the meat, stir in the wine, Worcestershire sauce, tomato sauce and season with salt and pepper

4. Bring to a boil, then reduce to a simmer

5. Simmer covered for at least 20 minutes

6. Serve with rice

BEEF SPRING ROLLS

Serves: **10**
Prep Time: **20**   Minutes

Cook Time: **30**   Minutes

Total Time: **40**   Minutes

INGREDIENTS

- 10 sheets spring roll pastry
- 2 tsp salt
- 2 tbs water
- 3 tbs pine nuts
- 1 ½ tsp black pepper
- 5 lb ground beef
- 3 tbs oil
- 2 tsp allspice
- 1 onion
- 1 ½ tbs flour

DIRECTIONS

1. Sauté the pine nuts in hot oil until golden
2. Chop the onion
3. Sauté the beef and add the onion, then season with salt, pepper and allspices
4. Sauté 5 more minutes until onions are soft
5. Place 2 tbs of the mixture in the center of a wrapper
6. Roll up fry in hot oil
7. Serve warm

LEMONY CAULIFLOWER

Serves: *4*
Prep Time: *10* Minutes

Cook Time: *20* Minutes

Total Time: *30* Minutes

INGREDIENTS

- 1 cauliflower
- 1 lemon
- Salt
- 3 tbs cornstarch

Sauce:

- 2 tsp lemon juice
- 1 garlic clove
- 3 tbs tahini

DIRECTIONS

1. Toss the cauliflower with cornstarch
2. Fry in hot oil for about 5 minutes
3. Mix the sauce ingredients together in a bowl

4. Serve the cauliflower with the sauce

ZUCCHINI BOATS

Serves: *4*
Prep Time: *10*   Minutes

Cook Time: *30*   Minutes

Total Time: *40*   Minutes

INGREDIENTS

- 2 zucchinis
- 1/3 tsp cinnamon
- 1 tsp nutmeg
- 1 tsp cardamom
- 2 tsp oregano
- 1 lb ground beef
- 1 onion
- 2 tsp garlic powder
- ½ cup water
- 4 tbs tahini paste
- 1 tsp ginger
- ½ tsp ground cloves
- ¼ tsp cayenne
- 1 tsp parsley

- 1 lemon
- 2 tsp salt

DIRECTIONS

1. Slice the zucchini lengthwise and scoop out the inside
2. Brush the halves with olive oil
3. Bake for at least 20 minutes until soft
4. Cook the beef and onions until done, then add in the lemon juice, tahini, spices and water
5. Fill the zucchinis with the meat mixture and heat in the oven for 5 minutes
6. Serve immediately

SPICED SQUID

Serves: **4**

Prep Time: **10** Minutes

Cook Time: **10** Minutes

Total Time: **20** Minutes

INGREDIENTS

- 50 g cornflour
- 2 tbs coriander
- 1 tsp black pepper
- 1 tsp allspices
- 2 tsp salt
- 650 g squid
- 2 tbs cayenne pepper
- 3 tbs cumin

DIRECTIONS

1. Cut the squid in rectangles and toss in cornflour, coriander, allspices, cumin, cayenne pepper, salt, and pepper
2. Fry in hot oil until golden

3. Serve sprinkled with salt

Serves: *4*
Prep Time: *10*   Minutes

Cook Time: *40*   Minutes

Total Time: *50*   Minutes

INGREDIENTS

- 30 oz chickpeas
- ¾ cup roasted red pepper
- 1 tsp red pepper flakes
- 2 bay leaves
- 4 tbs olive oil'3 tbs cumin
- 3 tbs tomato paste
- 2 lbs chicken thighs
- 3 tbs lemon juice
- 4 garlic cloves
- 2 cups bread cubes
- 4 tbs parsley leaves
- Salt

DIRECTIONS

1. Season the chicken with salt and cook until golden-brown

2. Cook the garlic for at least 30 seconds, then add tomato paste, cumin and red pepper flakes

3. Stir for about 1 minute

4. Add the chicken, bay leaves and 4 cups water

5. Bring to a boil, then simmer for about 20 minutes

6. Simmer the chickpeas for 5 minutes

7. Add the shredded chicken, red peppers, oil and lemon juice and simmer for 1 minute

8. Serve with bread cubes and season again if desired

DESSERTS

KNEFE

Serves: *8*

Prep Time: *20* Minutes

Cook Time: *40* Minutes

Total Time: *60* Minutes

INGREDIENTS

- 15 oz phyllo
- 1 egg
- 2 sticks butter
- 3 tbs sugar
- 1 ½ tsp lemon juice
- 15 oz ricotta cheese

Syrup:

- 2 tbs orange water
- 1 cup water
- 2 cups sugar

DIRECTIONS

1. Shred phyllo into a mixing bowl and add butter, then divide into two

2. Mix ricotta, sugar, egg and lemon juice together

3. Place a layer of phyllo on the bottom of a greased baking dish and add the ricotta mixture on top

4. Cover with the remaining phyllo and sprinkle with butter

5. Bake until golden and allow to cool

6. Place the water and sugar into a pot and simmer until it comes to a boil

7. Boil for 1 minute, then reduce the heat and add the orange water

8. Allow to cool

9. Serve the knefe drizzled with the syrup

TURMERIC CAKE

Serves: *16*
Prep Time: *10* Minutes

Cook Time: *20* Minutes

Total Time: *30* Minutes

INGREDIENTS

- **2 cups coarse semolina**
- **1 cup sugar**
- **2 tbs turmeric**
- **2 tbs baking powder**
- **¾ cup canola oil**
- **2 tbs tahini**
- **Almonds**
- **½ cup flour**
- **1 cup milk**

DIRECTIONS

1. **Mix the dry ingredients together**
2. **Mix the wet ingredients in a separate bowl**

3. Combine the two mixtures, mixing until smooth

4. Pour the batter into a greased baking pan and sprinkle almonds over

5. Bake in the preheated oven for at least 30 minutes at 350F

6. Serve cold

MEGHLI

Serves: *8*
Prep Time: *5*   Minutes

Cook Time: *25* Minutes

Total Time: *30* Minutes

INGREDIENTS

- 1 cup flour
- 1 ½ cups sugar
- ½ cup almonds
- 2 tbs anise seeds
- 8 cups water
- ½ cup pistachios
- 1/3 cup pine nuts
- 10 tsp shredded coconut
- ½ cup walnuts
- 1 tbs caraway powder
- 1 ½ tbs cinnamon powder

DIRECTIONS

1. Peel and soak the walnuts, almonds, pistachios and pine nuts in cold water
2. Mix the flour, caraway, sugar, anise and cinnamon together
3. Add the water and mix well
4. Put in the cooking pot on the stove and stir
5. Cook for at least 20 minutes
6. Pour into individual cups and allow to cool
7. Serve topped with coconuts and the nuts

PISTACHIO CAKE

Serves: **10**

Prep Time: **20** Minutes

Cook Time: **40** Minutes

Total Time: **60** Minutes

INGREDIENTS
Cake:
- 4 eggs
- 1 ½ cup Greek yogurt
- 2 tbs vanilla
- 1 ½ cups sugar
- 2 tsp baking powder
- 1 ½ cup flour
- 2 cups pistachios
- 1 tsp salt
- 2 sticks butter

Glaze:
- 3 tbs milk
- Salt
- ½ cup sugar
- 1/3 tsp ground cinnamon

DIRECTIONS

1. Whisk the eggs and sugar together using a mixer
2. Beat in the yogurt, butter and vanilla
3. Pulse the pistachios using a food processor
4. Sift the flour, ground pistachios, baking powder and salt in a bowl
5. Mix the wet and dry ingredients until smooth
6. Pour the batter into a prepared baking dish and cook in the preheated oven for at least 50 minutes at 325F
7. Mix the glaze ingredients together until smooth
8. Serve the cake drizzled with the glaze

Serves: **80**
Prep Time: **10**   Minutes

Cook Time: **10**   Minutes

Total Time: **20**   Minutes

INGREDIENTS

- 1 lb chocolate biscuit cookies
- 1 cup sugar
- 5 tbs cocoa powder
- 4 oz chocolate
- 1 cup butter
- 2 tsp instant coffee
- ½ cup milk

DIRECTIONS

1. Grind the biscuits using a food processor
2. Melt the chocolate and the butter together until smooth and well mixed
3. Combine the biscuit crumbs, melted chocolate, cocoa powder, coffee and sugar together

4. Slowly stir in the milk and continue mixing until smooth
5. Form balls from the dough, then roll the balls into powdered sugar, sprinkles, coconut flakes or sugar
6. Refrigerate until firm and serve

Serves: *4*
Prep Time: *10*   Minutes

Cook Time: *10*   Minutes

Total Time: *20*   Minutes

INGREDIENTS

- 15 apricots
- 1 cinnamon stick
- 150 g pudding rice
- 1/3 lemon
- 3 tsp rosewater
- 280 ml double cream
- 200 ml milk
- 3 tsp orange water
- 75 g pistachios
- 3 tbs sugar
- 2 vanilla pods

DIRECTIONS

1. Put the rice, cream, sugar, milk and vanilla in a pan
2. Bring to a boil, then simmer for at least 20 minutes
3. Place the dried apricots in water with the cinnamon stick and bring to a boil, then simmer for 10 minutes
4. Remove the vanilla pod and stir in the orange water
5. Divide into bowls and spoon apricots over
6. Serve topped with pistachios

MHALABIA

Serves: **4**
Prep Time: **5**   Minutes

Cook Time: **10**   Minutes

Total Time: **15**   Minutes

INGREDIENTS

- 4 cups milk
- 1 cup sugar
- 3 tsp rose water
- 1/3 cup maizena
- Pistachios

DIRECTIONS

1. Mix the maizena and sugar together until well combined
2. Add ¼ cup milk and stir until smooth
3. Heat the remaining milk until boiling point, then add the maizena mixture over and stir well
4. Cook for 5 minutes then remove from heat
5. Stir in the rose water and stir to combine

6. Pour into bowls and allow to cool
7. Refrigerate for at least 3 hours
8. Serve topped with crushed pistachios

SPICED PUDDING

Serves: **4**
Prep Time: **10** Minutes

Cook Time: **20** Minutes

Total Time: **30** Minutes

INGREDIENTS

- 3 cups water
- 1 tsp cinnamon
- 2 tsp caraway seeds
- 1 tsp aniseed
- 65 g flour
- ½ cup sugar

DIRECTIONS

1. Bring 2 cups of water to a boil
2. Whisk together 1 cup water with the flour until smooth
3. Mix the sugar and the spices in a bowl
4. Add the flour mixture to the boiling water and stir

5. Stir in ½ of the sugar mixture, stir, then add the remaining sugar mixture

6. Simmer for about 20 minutes, until it thickens

7. Serve cold

Serves: *2*
Prep Time: *5*   Minutes

Cook Time: *5*   Minutes

Total Time: *10* Minutes

INGREDIENTS

- 4 cups milk
- 1 cup sugar
- 2 tbs rose water
- 1 tbs sahlab

DIRECTIONS

1. Mix the sahlab with sugar
2. Pour the milk into a saucepan and add the sahlab mixture
3. Bring to a simmer and stir until thickened
4. Add the rosewater and continue stirring
5. Pour into cups and serve sprinkled with cinnamon